HOW TO BECOME A
SKILLFUL
INTERVIEWER

The WorkSmart Series

HOW TO BECOME A SKILLFUL INTERVIEWER

Randi Toler Sachs

amacom

AMERICAN MANAGEMENT ASSOCIATION
THE WORKSMART SERIES

New York • Atlanta • Boston • Chicago • Kansas City • San Francisco • Washington, D.C.
Brussels • Mexico City • Tokyo • Toronto

This book is available at a special
discount when ordered in bulk quantities.
For information, contact Special Sales Department,
AMACOM, a division of American Management Association,
135 West 50th Street, New York, NY 10020.

This publication is designed to provide accurate and authoritative
information in regard to the subject matter covered. It is sold with the
understanding that the publisher is not engaged in rendering legal,
accounting, or other professional service. If legal advice or other expert
assistance is required, the services of a competent professional person
should be sought.

Library of Congress Cataloging-in-Publication Data

Sachs, Randi Toler.
    How to become a skillful interviewer / Randi Toler Sachs.
       p. cm.—(The WorkSmart series)
    ISBN 0-8144-7831-X
    1. Employment interviewing. I. Title. II. Series.
HF5549.5.I6S23   1994
658.3'1124—dc20   94-4850
                                   CIP

Printing number

10 9 8 7 6 5 4 3 2 1

CONTENTS

HOW TO BECOME A
SKILLFUL
INTERVIEWER

INTRODUCTION

What's so hard about interviewing job applicants? After all, you have the superior position, and you have a job to offer. All you have to do is select which of the many people clamoring to be employed best suits you.

Most of the people you interview will be interested, enthusiastic, and eager to work at your place of business. Most will claim to have vast experience in just what it is you need them to have done, and they will profess a willingness and ability to learn any new skills that might be required of them.

Many of the job applicants will insist that money is not the deciding factor for them in seeking the ideal position. They will say they are more interested in opportunity, both to learn and to serve your specific needs.

With so many people like this to choose from, why is it that so many of us experience problems with new employees? Are they all lying through their teeth during the job interviews, or are we failing to ask the right questions?

The truth is that interviewing may appear to be simple, but *skillful* interviewing is not quite so simple. In order to interview effectively, you need to understand a great deal about the applicant. You want to learn about this individual's skills, abilities, interests, and experience. You also want to understand something about the individual's work style and personal style in order to determine if he will be able to work well with your staff. You even want to learn about the applicant's long- and short-term career goals—his actual goals, not the ones on his resumé. And in the process of interviewing the applicant, you also want to be able to make a good impression yourself because a hiring decision benefits

1

you equally as much as it does him. You don't want to scare away any potentially "perfect" employees.

This book will help you become aware of how you are interviewing job applicants now and what you can do to improve your skills in the process. As you read, think about how you would be naturally inclined to handle the situations described. Then consider how you could handle them better.

The positive side of interviewing is that each applicant presents an opportunity for you to hire an individual who may be a great addition to your staff. Unfortunately, the best person for the job may not be the most obvious. Sharpening your interviewing skills is the best way to improve your chances of hiring the best.

CHAPTER 1

WHAT IS AN EFFECTIVE INTERVIEW?

"Well, thank you for coming, we'll be in touch."

The manager stands and watches the job applicant leave. A few seconds later, her secretary comes in the office.

"Well, how was that one?" she asks.

"Not a real possibility," says the manager. "I'm really not sure why, but we just didn't click."

"No personality?" asks the secretary.

"No, I wouldn't say that. He was quite personable."

"Just didn't have the right qualifications then?"

"Actually, he was well-qualified," replies the manager.

"But you just didn't think he was right for the job," says the secretary.

"That's it. Well, I'll put his application aside just in case no one better comes along. When is the next interview scheduled?"

"Four o'clock this afternoon. I'll get you the resumé."

"Thanks a lot. I think this is going to take longer than I'd planned," says the manager.

Have you ever had an experience similar to this manager's? It's not uncommon for well-qualified job candidates to be dismissed from consideration because the person conducting the interview didn't get an instinctual feeling that the candidate would fit into the department. In fact, "getting a good

Getting a good feeling is probably one of the strongest deciding factors used in hiring.

feeling" about a job applicant is probably one of the strongest deciding factors used in making hiring selections. Certainly we all should give credit to our instincts, but it is not fair to ourselves or to the candidates we interview to make a selection based on this alone. Chances are that if the above manager reflected on how she conducted the interview she would realize that she had not given the candidate a fair chance.

What do you want to accomplish in an interview? What makes an interview effective? For our definition, let us say that *an effective interview is one in which you have successfully explored a job applicant's suitability for the position available.* An effective interview gives you some insight into the candidate's work style and her strengths and weaknesses, and one in which you have given the applicant an accurate representation of the position, the company as a whole, and the role that she will be expected to play as a member of your department.

You may get the most talkative applicant, not the best qualified.

Notice that according to this definition, responsibility for success has been placed in the interviewer's hands. All too often, managers (especially those for whom interviewing is an occasional event) expect a job applicant to take the lead and make an impression on them. But this may guarantee only that you get the most talkative applicant, not the best qualified. By reading this book, you've taken the first step toward improving your interviewing skills and technique. You've recognized that it is up to you to set the agenda for the interview and to elicit all the information you need to make an informed, intelligent hiring decision.

An effective hiring interview has six basic elements:

1. *It has an agenda.* You can't expect to read an employee's resumé, match it up to the job description you've prepared, and then take it from there. If the job being filled is important, your attention to preparing an agenda is time well-spent.

2. *It obtains information critical to your making a hiring*

decision. Don't allow yourself to get so caught up in conversation that you neglect to get the facts you need.

3. *It gives the applicant a chance to demonstrate her knowledge, technical ability, and problem-solving skills.* Rather than just going over what is listed on the resumé, a skillful interviewer asks probing questions that allow an applicant to show whether she has the qualities that make her right for the job.

An effective interview gives the applicant a chance to demonstrate knowledge, ability, and problem solving.

4. *It is led by the interviewer but is flexible enough to change direction to accommodate the applicant.* All applicants for the same position do not have to be interviewed in exactly the same manner. Sticking to an agenda does not preclude allowing the applicant to discuss other subjects as well.

5. *It asks all questions in a nondiscriminatory manner.* Managers must be aware of what constitutes an inappropriate or discriminatory question.

6. *It gives the applicant a truthful understanding of what the job entails.* There is no greater waste of time than hiring an employee who quits soon after because the job did not meet her expectations.

Conducting hiring interviews is one of the many responsibilities that come with the territory of becoming a manager or supervisor. For almost all of us, our ability to perform this task was not the reason for our being given it; it is just part of the package deal. Like it or not, though, hiring good employees is a crucial factor in the success or failure of your department. It is well worth your effort to learn how to do this particular task skillfully and knowledgeably.

IS IT YOUR FAULT?

How do you know whether an interview went poorly because of the applicant's lack of ability or because of your failure to do your job well? Consider the following warning signs that demonstrate the need for you to reevaluate and work on improving your interviewing technique:

□ The applicant had all the qualifications on his resumé but did not have an opportunity to expand on them during the interview.

□ Questions about the applicant's work experience remain unanswered at the end of the interview.

□ You realize you know more about the applicant's personal life and likes and dislikes than you do her professional background.

□ The applicant takes the initiative in ending the interview.

□ You have not had enough time to cover all aspects of the position during the interview.

□ You discussed many different subjects but nothing in any depth.

□ You were not able to put the applicant at ease during the entire interview.

□ You have obtained little evidence to support the applicant's claims of proficiency and knowledge.

□ You learned a good deal about the applicant but do not have a clear sense of whether he would be right for the position you need to fill.

If you can identify a number of these situations after a typical interview, don't despair. Recognize that interviewing employee applicants is not something that comes naturally to anyone. There is a lot more to the task than simply to hold a conversation with the applicant and try to obtain information. Read on, and continue to test yourself in order to gain insight into how to conduct effective employment interviews.

IT'S NOT A CHAT

One of the most common mistakes that inexperienced interviewers make is to treat an employment interview as if it were a getting-acquainted chat. The following questions are typical of such an interview; each can be answered too easily with a response that gives you little concrete information. After each example, jot down how you could ask that question in a more effective manner. Try to construct your questions in such a way that the candidate has no choice but to give you useful information. The first two are filled in to get you started:

Chat: So, tell me about yourself.
Interview: Can you tell me how you came to enter this field and what specifically you've been doing recently?

Chat: How did you like your college courses in engineering?
Interview: What was your academic field of concentration in engineering? Do you feel you draw heavily on this background or that you've learned more from experience?

Chat: What's your current job like?
Interview: _____

_____

_____

_____

Chat: What's your idea of a perfect job?
Interview: _____

_____

_____

_____

Chat: What do you think are your biggest strengths and weaknesses?
Interview: _____

_____

_____

_____

Chat: Do you enjoy traveling on business?
Interview: _____

_____

_____

_____

Chat: Why do you want to work for our company?
Interview: _____

_____

_____

_____

The preceding exercise will start you thinking about how and why the questions you ask during an employment interview are different from those you ask someone in a friendly conversation. Chapter 2 will help you think about your own style of interviewing in greater depth.

CHAPTER 2

WHAT'S YOUR INTERVIEWING IMAGE?

It is usually the most unpleasant and oddest interviewers who are remembered.

If you are new to interviewing, you've probably sat on the other side of the desk answering questions more times than you've been the one to ask them. But even if you are an experienced interviewer, you can surely recall some of the more memorable interviews that you endured during one job search or another. Usually the most unpleasant and the oddest interviewers are the ones who leave indelible marks on our memories. Let us assume that you would rather be remembered for giving fair, intelligent, and interesting interviews.

Before examining the content of what to say in an interview, consider the image that you present. If that image is too strong one way or another—it can get in the way of a productive session with a promising job applicant. Here are two examples:

Heather's office is cluttered. Books are crammed into shelves haphazardly, and the in-basket and out-basket flow into one another on her desk. In fact, there is very little space on her desk that remains uncovered at all. When job applicants enter her office, Heather has to clear off a chair so that they can sit down. She usually has little choice but to dump what was on the chair onto the floor next to her desk. If Heather is lucky, she can usually locate the resumé under the pile on her desk. Once she does that, she can sit down and begin getting to know the applicant.

Vanessa's office is extremely neat. In fact, an outsider might think that Vanessa does not get too involved in the work of her department, preferring to do a great deal of delegation rather than get her hands dirty, so to speak. When job applicants enter her office, she is seated at her desk with just a resumé and a pencil in front of her. She offers candidates a seat in an armless chair that is precisely centered in the room, a few feet away from the desk.

Idiosyncrasies that are too prominent can serve to prejudice applicants needlessly.

Both Heather and Vanessa project strong images to job applicants just by the way they keep their offices. Heather's office may be off-putting to a candidate who might worry that this manager is not organized enough to consider all the candidates fairly by their qualifications. A job applicant might wonder if Heather will even be able to find his resumé again once the interview is over. Vanessa gives an austere impression and magnifies it by seating the interviewee in a rather vulnerable-feeling position. A seat without arms that is spaced apart from any other furniture can make an individual feel as though he is on display. Vanessa may actually scare away potentially good employees who fear that she will be a supervisor who is very difficult to please or hard to approach for help or direction.

Even if both Heather and Vanessa have wonderful interviewing styles, each has an image to overcome. It is important to remember that you must also make a good impression on candidates. The employment interview can be the start of a long working relationship. But idiosyncrasies that are too prominent can serve to prejudice applicants needlessly about the type of person you might be to work for.

ASSESS YOUR OFFICE

Look at your own office or workstation. Are there any distractions that might hamper holding a successful interview? Is this the image you want to present to potential employees? If not, here are some suggestions on how you can make easy changes without compromising your individuality.

Situation	Problem	Change
Disorganized office	Gives poor impression of manager	Straighten up office before applicant enters
Austere office	Makes applicants uncomfortable	Rearrange furniture for better conversation; add a few personal items for warmth
Open office workstation	Lacks privacy	Conduct interview in a closed office or make certain applicant is not facing open partition; arrange for coworkers to leave communal office space during interview
Outside noise	Impedes conversation	Close windows; use fan if necessary
Office filled with personal items (photos, memorabilia, etc.)	Distracts from business of interview	Limit number of photos. Do not display political, religious, or ethnic items unless they are directly related to business
Shabby furnishings, old equipment	Gives impression of company unwilling to invest in comfort of employees	Eliminate unnecessary clutter and furnishings; request paint job; add an interesting wall hanging or calendar to distract the eye

LOOK IN THE MIRROR

Take a few minutes to look in the mirror and determine if you're satisfied with the image that you personally are presenting. Although you may feel that you've earned the right to relax and not have to fuss with your appearance, when interviewing potential employees it is wise to take some extra care with your grooming. The rule to follow is simple: Dress neatly and appropriately to the business you are in. Avoid high-fashion and faddish clothes that draw too much attention to what you are wearing and may take away from what you have to say.

FIRST IMPRESSIONS

Now that you've assessed your office and are satisfied with the appearance you make, think about the impression you are making with your interviewing style. First impressions are generally the strongest, so let's look at how an interviewer's opening statement can set the tone.

In the exercise that follows, put yourself in the applicant's seat. What would you think about the opening statement made by each of these managers? Would you feel comfortable—or not? Would the statement give you hope that the interview would be successful?

Eric: Come in and sit down. I see by your resumé that you have the minimum qualifications required for this job. Tell me, why should I hire you?
Your response: _____

_____

_____

_____

Sue: So nice to meet you. Please make yourself comfortable. As you know we're trying to fill an opening for a marketing associate.
Your response: _____

_____

_____

_____

_____

Jim: Come right in. I've looked over your resumé, and I can see you've had some good experience for this job. Why don't you tell me about yourself while I fix a cup of coffee. Would you like a cup, too?
Your response: _____

_____

_____

_____

_____

Trudy: Hello. It's good to meet you. I hope the directions we gave you were okay. I'd like to begin by finding out more about your experience in direct marketing. In your resumé you say that you've been involved in an ongoing campaign for two years now. Can you tell me what this entails?
Your response: _____

_____

_____

_____

_____

Which of the four interviewers, if any, come closest to your style of beginning an interview? Let's analyze what each of them is doing with the opening remarks.

Eric is presenting a challenging demeanor. If his intention is to weed out any employees who are hesitant or have less than 100 percent self-confidence, then he is taking the right tack. But Eric (and all interviewers who believe in a confrontation-style approach) should be aware that the most confident interviewee is not always the most competent employee. Eric is also giving a strong impression of a tough manager who may not be easy to work for.

Sue is taking the opposite approach. Her low-key manner is so unintimidating that she fails to ask a question and lead the interview. She makes a statement about the job opening and leaves it up to the applicant to fill in what he believes would be a good way to get the discussion rolling. The applicant may wonder whether Sue has even examined his resumé. Again, only the most confident applicant will successfully prevail with an interviewer who fails to take control—no matter how gentle the interviewer's manner may be.

Jim is playing the role of Mr. Friendly. He tries to put the applicant at ease by making a positive opening statement and offering a cup of coffee. His is not a very conventional or business-like approach, but it can be effective if he settles down and follows up the coffee by getting down to the business of interviewing. However, if Jim takes the rest of the interview as casually as he does its beginning, the applicant is likely to believe that she is not a serious candidate or that Jim is not disciplined enough to evaluate applicants on their qualifications. Instead, the applicant may get the impression that the person with the best personality will be the one who gets hired.

Trudy is the only interviewer who makes no apologies for conducting a serious interview while remaining friendly and cordial. She quickly gets down to business by announcing her intention of learning specific information and then follows it up with a question demonstrating that she is well-prepared for the interview. She also chooses to begin with a question that the applicant should feel comfortable answering because it concerns his current position. Trudy can ask more challenging questions later in the interview.

What type of first impression do you make? Are you able to set the tone for a productive session from the beginning? Keep in mind that the most effective interviews are the ones in which you are able to evaluate an applicant's suitability to the job honestly. Setting up situations that arbitrarily challenge the applicant or abdicate your own responsibility to uncover the information you need will not help you achieve the goal of hiring the best possible employee.

In summary, there are three key factors within your control that can strongly affect the interviews that you conduct.

1. *Your work space.* Where you conduct employment interviews can have an influence over what is accomplished. Make the effort to portray an image that is appropriate for your organization and your industry.

2. *Your appearance.* Prepare yourself on the outside as well as internally to make a good impression when meeting potential employees.

3. *Your interview approach.* Don't play a role by trying to confront applicants unnecessarily or by trying to come across as a friend or confidant rather than as an interviewer. Help yourself and your applicants by preparing relevant questions that allow them to demonstrate their qualifications for the position. Remember that the way you begin an interview can set the tone for the entire meeting. Your objective should be to make the applicant comfortable while sticking to the purpose of the interview.

CHAPTER 3

HOW ARE YOU INFLUENCED?

Carolyn is a well-dressed black woman of 35.

Thomas is a tall Caucasian man, age 42. He dresses casually but expensively.

Meredith is a matronly looking woman of 50.

Dorothy is age twenty-four and dresses in very high-fashion clothing.

Edwin's resumé states that he has a degree from Harvard.

David is a thirty-six-year-old Caucasian who is 5 feet, 3 inches tall.

Jeff is the thirty-nine-year-old manager who must interview each of these job applicants for a publicity writer's position. Do you think he will have any hunches on who would be best for the job based on this information alone?

The truth is that most people gravitate toward others who are most like themselves.

In a perfect world—but an emotional vacuum perhaps—Jeff would have little, if nothing, to influence him when interviewing these persons. But in a real situation, Jeff's subconscious may already be making choices and judgments based on such arbitrary factors as appearance, age, height, and race. The truth is that most people, consciously or not, gravitate toward others who are most like themselves. Therefore, the greater the differences are between the applicant and the interviewer, the greater is the challenge for the interviewer to be an objective evaluator.

The law attempts to protect people from prejudice based on such characteristics. (We will discuss this in greater detail in Chapter 8.) But restrictions on what we can and cannot say go only so far. It is impossible to regulate how we feel. It is, however, advisable to become aware of what influences you when you are interviewing a job candidate so that you can work on overcoming any prejudices that may serve to disqualify good candidates.

Reread the list of potential job applicants at the beginning of the chapter. Do you automatically picture someone for each description? How do you expand upon the character? Are there other characteristics that you assume go hand in hand with the ones already mentioned?

Take David, for example. At 5 feet, 3 inches, he is noticeably short. Would his height make a difference in how you view him as a job candidate? Do terms such as *plucky, weak,* or *Napoleonic complex* come to mind when you meet a man of David's height?

Edwin is the candidate with the degree from Harvard. Do you automatically give him the edge? "Well, why not?" you say. "He's proved that he's exceptionally smart if he can get through Harvard." That's true. A degree from an Ivy League school should count for something. It can even count for a lot. However, we caution against your letting it count for everything. There are many factors to consider in making a hiring selection and you should be sure not to let a major advantage cloud your judgment about additional considerations.

What pushes your buttons? Are you aware of having any "red flag" feelings about certain types of job applicants? When you think of the perfect job candidate, do you include such characteristics as age, gender, appearance, race, religion, personality, or marital status? All of these factors can lead us to stereotype a candidate and deny that person a fair interview.

One way you can fight this tendency toward stereotyping is to do a little self-education. To avoid falling into the trap of prejudging others, remember that each candidate you meet is a unique individual who should not have to be handicapped because of your own biases. In fact, for every stereotype you can think of, you can probably also think of one or several other people who defy that stereotype. Is it not logical that if you know one person who defies that description, then you should give the job applicants you interview the same benefit of the doubt?

Try the following exercise. For each stereotypical conclusion you might draw about a job candidate, think of someone you know who does not fit that description.

An applicant over age 50. Typical prejudgments include: not able to take change well; less knowledgeable about computers and other office technology; more concerned about retirement benefits than growth potential.
But what about? . . . _____

_____?

A minority college graduate. Typical prejudgments include: Went to school on a minority quota; won't be willing to start at bottom; won't get along well with coworkers.
But what about? . . . _____

_____?

A poorly dressed applicant. Typical prejudgments include: Careless about work; unable to keep current with changes; negligent about detail-oriented work.
But what about? . . . _____

_____?

A strikingly attractive applicant. Typical prejudgments include: Gets by on his looks; expects special attention/dispensation from others; not as intelligent; less competent and less hard working.
But what about? . . . _____

_____?

Can you come up with enough exceptions to these stereotypes to demonstrate how dangerous it can be to remain unaware of them? Competent job applicants come in all shapes, sizes, ages, and ethnic backgrounds. Put your prejudices aside before you begin an interview, and concentrate on matching an applicant's capabilities and work style to the position you need to fill.

CHAPTER 4

PREPARING FOR
THE HIRING INTERVIEW

"Now, let me just take a look at your resumé, and we'll
   begin."
"Where are you working at the present time?"
"From what school did you graduate?"
"Have you had any supervisory experience?"
"Where were you working before this job?"

What do all of these interview questions have in common?
They all demonstrate that the interviewer failed to prepare
adequately for the hiring interview. An effective interviewer
does not waste time asking questions that have already been
answered in writing. It's essential to prepare in advance for
the interview by reading the resumé or application, or both,
thoroughly and then putting together questions according
to what information you need to evaluate the applicant.

These preparations begin well before you read resumés—in
fact, even before you announce any job opening. The first
step is to do a thorough analysis of the open position.

**You must
do a thor-
ough analy-
sis of the
open posi-
tion.**

ANALYZING YOUR NEEDS

Too often, when an employee gives notice, the supervisor's
reflex is to dig into the files and pull out that employee's job
description. After a quick read and perhaps a change or two,
the supervisor then sends it down to personnel with a request
to run an ad to attract candidates for the job. If the supervisor
is lucky, the personnel associate will question whether the

description is still accurate. Consider the following scenario as an example:

Personnel: We just received your request for a new administrative assistant. I'd like to go over a few things with you before I run the ad.

Manager: Well, if you want. But I think you can probably run the same ad as last time. He was only here for four years.

Personnel: Let's see if things have changed. The old ad reads: *Administrative Assistant for busy department. Responsibilities include correspondence, word processing, support services for four salespeople. Ability to work independently important.* How does that sound to you now?

Manager: Actually, there are a few more requirements for the job now. The candidate should have experience in desktop publishing in addition to word processing. There are now six salespeople to support, and I'd really like to find someone who speaks Spanish as well.

Personnel: It's a good thing we talked. I'll rewrite the ad and beginning looking through the resumés that we have on file.

When a position opens up, particularly through turnover, it is a great opportunity to reevaluate what is needed to fill that void. Often some of the responsibilities that the departing employee filled can be given to lower-level employees, who will appreciate the chance to take on new tasks that will help them to improve their skills and marketability. Before any recruiting is done is the time to determine what place in the department this individual will fill. That is not to say that you cannot alter this decision if an applicant with more to offer turns up, but you must know what you are looking for before you begin the search process.

Actually, there are three issues to address here:

1. You must determine what the exact job responsibilities of the new employee will be; in other words,

you must define the job and prepare a profile of the position.

2. You must determine what qualifications and skills are required in order to be able to carry out those responsibilities.

3. You should determine if the job requires a specific type of personality or temperament in an individual so that you can prepare an "ideal candidate profile." Do you need someone outgoing, for example, or is a more introverted type better suited to the position?

You can use the following questionnaire to make sure you have covered all the aspects of the job.

EMPLOYEE REQUIREMENTS

Employee title: _____

Employee is responsible for: _____

_____

_____

_____

_____

_____

Employee reports to: _____

_____

Employee works cooperatively with following staff members: _____

_____

_____

_____

Employee should be knowledgeable about: _____

_____

_____

_____

_____

Employee should have practical work experience in the following: _____

_____

_____

_____

_____

Formal education/degrees/certification/license required: _____

_____

_____

Computer/technology skills required: _____

_____

_____

_____

_____

Amount of overtime expected: _____

Amount of travel expected: _____

Salary range to be offered: _____

This form can be used not only to prepare a classified ad or provide information for an employment agency or personnel department; it can also be used to assess resumés and applications for job suitability. Determining from the resumé whether an individual meets your qualifications is not always

Sometimes the way a resumé is worded makes it difficult to get to the details you need.

easy or straightforward. Sometimes the way a resumé is worded, for example, makes it difficult to get to the details you need. This questionnaire can help you take apart the resumé bit by bit and make a more accurate judgment after analyzing the information.

For most position vacancies, ask candidates to fill out a job application. It can elicit educational background, job history, the candidate's social security number (which can be used to check references), and starting and ending salaries in past and present positions—information that is useful to you but generally is not included in a resumé. The application is a less awkward way to acquire this information than verbal questions, which may be uncomfortable for some people.

EXAMINING A RESUMÉ

Resumés, presented as a job applicant's work and educational history, are really word puzzles that you need to decipher and interpret. Remember that everything in a resumé is written to show the applicant in the best light. Your job is to try to uncover as much of the truth as you possibly can. You are limited, however, by an individual's right to privacy and by questions that can be considered discriminatory, topics covered in greater detail in Chapter 8.

When reading a resumé, look out for the following:

- ☐ Gaps in dates of employment. This often indicates a period of unemployment. What is the reason for the gap? You have the right to ask.
- ☐ Companies listed that are no longer in business. Can you verify that the company did indeed exist at the time indicated on the resumé?
- ☐ Exaggerating the usefulness of training courses. Did the applicant attend a legitimate course that taught a new skill, or was it a

weekend seminar that gave an overview of a topic?

☐ Claims that the applicant "supervised" or "managed" a project team. How many people were on this team? Could it have actually been an independent project?

☐ Listing years of experience that do not match the years actually spent in the work force.

☐ Job changes that do not indicate advancement.

☐ Exaggerated job titles that are meant to impress.

☐ A large number of relocations for which the applicant offers no explanation.

☐ References that all come from out of town. Unless the applicant has only recently moved to your area, this could indicate that she has something to hide.

All resumés should be read thoroughly before the interview takes place. Feel free to underline or circle any items in it about which you would like to ask. Ask yourself the following about the resumé:

☐ Does it give a clear picture of the applicant's work experiences, present and past?

☐ Does it list the applicant's educational background, and are your requirements met?

☐ Are there any skills you require that are not mentioned on the resumé?

☐ Is there any contradictory information on the resumé? Be sure to ask about that.

☐ Does the available position seem to be a natural move for the applicant? Why?

Any major omission in a resumé is probably a good enough reason to decide against granting an interview. If you decide to go ahead and interview someone with a questionable resumé, be prepared to obtain the information the applicant has failed to provide. If the omission is a deal breaker—that is, you cannot consider hiring the candidate without the specific qualification that has not been listed—ask the candidate about this on the telephone before committing to an interview.

SETTING AN AGENDA

By reading the applicant's resumé and comparing it with the Employee Requirements questionnaire, you have taken the first steps toward setting an agenda for an effective interview. Next, you must devise a plan for how to question the applicant in order to obtain the information you need.

Assuming the resumé or application submitted was thorough and straightforward, let's look at what information you have and what you don't.

You Probably Know:

- Current and past job titles held by the applicant
- Types of businesses in which the applicant has worked
- Years of experience in the field
- Technical skills claimed by the applicant
- Formal education, degrees, licenses
- Additional education and training

You Still Need to Know:

- Actual responsibilities held by the applicant
- Applicant's approach to work
- Applicant's objectives in seeking new employment
- Applicant's short- and long-term goals
- Applicant's compatibility (work style plus skill level) with your own department members
- Applicant's actual skill level

Every employment interview should have a definite beginning, a middle, and an end, and you need to prepare yourself to carry out the meeting in this structure.

The beginning of the interview serves as an introduction. Welcome the applicant cordially, and direct her to a seat that has been set up for her. Many interviewers like to start off with an innocuous icebreaking remark about the applicant's travel or the weather. You can then take the opportunity to tell the applicant that you have reviewed her resumé and are looking forward to finding out more about her—an easy transition to asking some probing questions.

PLANNING YOUR QUESTIONS

The main part of the interview will focus on asking questions of the applicant that are designed to reveal her actual job qualifications and give you the information you need as to whether this person will be a match for the job. When you prepared for the interview by reading the applicant's resumé and/or application carefully, you planned your questions.

There is nothing wrong with having a list of prepared questions, but if you don't like the idea of reading questions, you can just list the subjects you want to cover. This alternative can work as long as you know what to ask in order to get the answers you need. In either case—prepared questions or a topic outline—plan to take notes during or directly after the interview—or both times. It is too easy to forget an impression made or an idea expressed by a job applicant, particularly when you are conducting multiple interviews and you forget which candidate said what.

During the interview, be prepared to listen. Keep your questions short and to the point so that the applicant has time to reply fully.

If there are any discrepancies or contradictions in information or dates listed in the resumé, you may want to ask about them early in the interview. In this way, you can clear up any concerns and be better able to concentrate on learning about the applicant's qualifications for the job.

An employment interview has a lot going on beneath the surface. Your goal is to find out as much about the applicant as you can, including any faults or shortcomings. The applicant, however, is determined to answer each question in a way that will show him in only the most favorable light.

ARE YOU READY?

Before beginning any employment interview, go over the following checklist to make sure you have properly prepared for the session:

☐ My office is neat and presentable.

☐ I have read and taken notes about the resumé and job application and have them on the desk.

☐ I have arranged not to be disturbed for the time allotted for the interview.

☐ I have arranged the furniture in a manner suitable for our discussion.

☐ I have a copy of the job description of the position available.

☐ I have available samples of the company's [or department's] work to show the applicant.

☐ I have prepared questions that are designed to elicit the specific information I need in order to make a fair evaluation.

DO YOU KNOW WHO YOU WANT?

Before you begin any interview, draw up a profile of the person you believe would be best in the position. Use the following checklist to make sure you know just what type of person is desired.

☐ I know the responsibilities of the job.

☐ I have identified the persons with whom the new employee will work.

☐ I have decided on the educational and experience requirements for the job.

☐ I have determined whether the job requires an individual with a specific type of temperament.

☐ I have clarified the salary range I may offer.

CHAPTER 5

ASKING THE RIGHT QUESTIONS

It is very easy for the perfect candidate to go unrecognized because the interviewer fails to ask the right questions.

Effective interviewing is not difficult or complicated, but it does have to be deliberate. The truth is that the perfect candidate may go unrecognized if the interviewer fails to ask the right questions.

Recall that an interview usually consists of three parts:

1. The beginning, devoted to getting acquainted and understanding how the applicant's qualifications match the requirements of the job
2. The main part of the interview, used to explore the applicant's work style, ideas, problem-solving abilities, unique strengths, and compatibility to the organization
3. The conclusion, used to discuss details about the company and the position and to answer questions the applicant may have

Many managers like to use the beginning of the interview to explain the position in greater detail to the applicant, but I advise you to proceed very cautiously with this. It only follows that the more you tell the applicant about your own needs and the way your workplace operates, the better he will be able to tailor his answers to fit your needs. Instead, plan on filling in the applicant with more about the job toward the end of the interview. If by that point you have a strong feeling that you are not going to hire this applicant, you do not have to spend much time discussing the job.

Begin each interview with a friendly greeting and a few remarks to put the applicant at ease and allow her a chance to settle in and look around. Then ask the applicant a question that is clearly based on information provided in the resumé—for example, about the applicant's present work and background as they pertain to the open position. When you have established some basic information about the applicant, the next questions you pose can be designed for her to demonstrate her knowledge, skills, or problem-solving ability.

In all employment interviews, it is important to take notes. Do applicants the courtesy of informing them that you will be taking notes—for example, "You don't mind my taking notes?"

Ed Schwartz, the manager of corporate employment, compensation, and employer relations of Parsons Brinkerhoff, a leading transportation engineering design firm, is an expert on employment interviewing. He advises interviewers of two important rules in employment interviewing:

1. Always remember the job you are interviewing for.
2. All questions must be job related.

These rules may seem simple enough, but it is quite easy to forget them and make some common interviewing mistakes, which can lead to hiring mistakes.

All interviewing requires the use of two different types of questions:

1. *Fact-gathering questions.* You may want to get these questions out of the way early. Did the resumé omit some important information? Questions about a professional license, certification, or fluency in another language can be answered yes or no and may be very important to your final decision making. Some fact-gathering questions should be asked to screen candidates over the telephone even before an interview is granted. These include essential requirements

such as relocation, ability to drive, experience in using specific equipment or software, or any other requirement of the job that cannot be overlooked.

2. *Open-ended questions.* Most questions will be open-ended; they require the applicant to go into depth with the answer. These types of questions don't have an obvious right or wrong. They are used to explore information on the resumé, such as "Tell me about this project you worked on at your last job," and to learn more about the applicant's attitudes, ideas, and future plans, such as "If you accepted this position, where would you like it to take you ultimately in your career?"

> **Open-ended questions encourage candidates to offer their ideas, aspirations, and opinions.**

Skillful interviewers avoid asking closed questions that serve to suppress the opportunity to learn more about the candidate. For example, asking "Do you know much about managing a pet shop?" will not yield as much information had you asked, "Tell me what you know about managing a pet shop—for example, how you manage sanitation and feeding schedules."

Because open-ended questions encourage candidates to offer their ideas, aspirations, and opinions, the interviewer must be able to evaluate the answers *as they relate to the job vacancy.* This is where many interviewers falter. It is difficult not to be influenced by answers that may be clever or interesting, display ambition, or offer great insight into the speaker. But in order to hire successfully, you need to be able to determine whether the answer tells you that the individual is right for the job—not right for the good of humanity or right for a potential friend for yourself.

THREE TYPES OF INTERVIEW

Let's examine some sample questions geared toward the three basic types of positions you may need to fill: (1) entry-level or college recruiting, (2) middle-level jobs that require a number of years of experience, and (3) executive recruitment.

College Recruiting

In recruiting recent college graduates, what you are really buying is potential. Grades are certainly a strong consideration, but the job does not always go to the candidate with the best grade point average. Interviewers should pay attention to whether the student worked during college, what types of courses the student took as electives, and any extracurricular activities that demonstrated abilities such as leadership, organizational skills, teamwork, or persistence.

The following questions are good to ask during college recruitment interviews:

> "How did you select your major field of study? Has it met your expectations?"
>
> "What are your immediate career goals? What type of job would you most like to obtain now?"
>
> "Can you tell me about your long-term career goals? What plan have you made regarding how to achieve them?"
>
> "What, besides your coursework, has prepared you for a position in this field?"
>
> "How have you spent your summers during college?"
>
> "Do you prefer teamwork or working independently?"
>
> "Have you considered graduate school? Will you be planning on continuing your education in the future?"
>
> "How did you choose your college? Were you happy with your choice?"
>
> "Why did you want to interview with our company?"

Add your own favorite questions for college recruiting:

_____

_____

_____

_____

_____

_____

In most interviews, you will find that something the applicant says leads you to ask a question that you did not plan on and takes you down a different path. Be aware of when you are digressing from a line of questioning and return to what you want to ask when you have learned enough about the alternative subject.

In recruiting college graduates, especially, it is hard not to be enchanted by the personable, aggressive interviewee. Many recent graduates are enthusiastic and brimming over with potential. They may try their hardest to sell themselves with words, because they lack the experience that they so wish to accumulate. I caution you, though, to bear in mind the position for which you are interviewing. It may be that a candidate with a different personality type is better suited to the position.

Looking for Experience

Filling a position that has been previously held and requires some solid experience requires different kinds of questions and a different approach to interviewing. Potential is no longer what you are looking for. At this point, you want the candidate to prove what he has achieved and you want to know if that is applicable to the job you are trying to fill. The questions are no longer based on "What would you do when . . . ?" but, rather, on "What do you do when . . . ?"

Suppose you are interviewing an applicant for a sales position. Which of the following questions do you think would be most effective to learn something about the applicant's selling style:

1. "What do you like most about selling?"
2. "Where did you get your best practical experience?"
3. "Which type of situation do you find most challenging?"
4. "Describe the types of sales pitches or programs you find most effective with your customers."

5. "Tell me about any special techniques you have for landing difficult sales."
6. "How do you handle a product that won't move?"

Although questions 1, 2, and 3 are all valid ones, the answers to 4, 5, and 6 are bound to reveal more about what the applicant has to offer. These questions give the applicant the opportunity to tell you something unique about his own style of selling. Unless you have the opportunity to observe the applicant in action, this is probably the best you can do to judge his qualifications. The cardinal rule here is: *Ask questions that require the applicant to demonstrate proved ability or original thought.*

An experienced candidate by definition is not new to the work force, so it is important to try to get a sense of how that person would fit into your work team. You should be very interested in how an individual approaches work and the attitude that she brings to it. You also need to think about the people who already work in your department when you are seeking another team member.

Let's look at the difference your questions can make in conducting an effective interview. As an example, Ray and Gabe are editors of trade magazines published by the same company. Each editor is interviewing for an associate editor whose duties include writing, research, and some production work. The personnel department is recruiting candidates and has sent Daniel to both of the editors to be interviewed. Although the job requirements for each magazine are virtually the same, the interviews strongly reflect the differences in the two editors.

First, Ray interviewed Daniel for his monthly magazine on the gourmet food industry.

Ray: I see by your resumé that you've been writing for local community newspapers for the past four years. Do you think you'd be happy working for a trade journal? You know, you wouldn't have a chance to do too many human interest stories, and hard news is, well, limited to industry news.

Daniel: Oh, that doesn't bother me. I feel I've had my fill of that type of reporting. I'd like to cover one industry in depth.

Ray: Do you know anything about the food industry?

Daniel: Well, I certainly like to eat. Umm, actually no, but I think it would be very interesting.

Ray: I don't imagine you did any production work on the newspapers, did you? Don't they have a layout and pasteup staff for that?

Daniel: Yes. They do have a staff that handles that, but I've always been interested in watching what they do. I think I could learn that pretty fast. In fact, I did do some of that in college.

Ray: We have a pretty small staff here. I need someone who is going to be able to work independently on his own projects and also cooperatively on staff projects.

Daniel: That sounds fine to me. I've always considered myself to be motivated and cooperative.

Next, Gabe interviewed Daniel for his monthly publication covering the nursing home field.

Gabe: I'd like to ask you an important question up front. Are you truly interested in moving from newspaper reporting to monthly trade journalism, or are you primarily concerned with making a move from your present job?

Daniel: Actually, I really would like to move to magazine writing. I know that trade journals don't have as much so-called glamour as do newspapers—even community papers—but I would like to concentrate on one field for reporting. I also think I would like the pace and the overall involvement on a monthly trade magazine better. I did work on this type of magazine while I was a college student, and I liked it very much.

Gabe: Tell me about that experience.

Daniel: It was just for one semester, but since I went to school in the state capitol, I was given a chance to work on a magazine that was distributed primarily to legislators and lobbyists. I liked how everyone on the staff worked together to put out an issue, but they still had their separate assignments to work on. At the newspaper, you pretty much write up the story you are assigned, hand it in, and walk away. Involvement is limited there.

Gabe asked a very important question—whether the job was truly of interest to Daniel or if he was mainly trying to get away from his present job and this position was the closest possibility to come along—and he did it much more successfully than Ray. Ray used a somewhat negative and closed manner of questioning, which resulted in inhibiting Daniel from bringing up his related work experience. Gabe managed to bring it out in the open and also to discover that Daniel has some of the important qualifications they are seeking. Gabe picked up on Daniel's related work experience and asked him to expound on it. Ray chose not to follow up and moved onto another question instead.

Interview questions for experienced candidates can be grouped according to three categories: (1) educational background and training, (2) past and present job experiences, and (3) future plans and aspirations. Here are some sample questions that can be used in most interviews:

Education and Training

Assuming that the candidate's resumé and/or application includes information about schools attended and degrees, licenses, and certification earned, the following questions can also be useful:

> "Do you have any plans to continue your education?"
> "How did your education prepare you for your career?"
> "What was the most useful training course(s) you've taken?"
> "Would you change anything about your education now that you've been in this field?"

"What training courses would you like to take in the future?"

Add questions pertaining to your specific field:

_____

_____

_____

_____

_____

Past and Present Job Experiences

In addition to asking about specific things on the applicant's resumé for clarification and elaboration, the following questions can give you useful information:

"Tell me about your current job. What do you do in a typical day?"

"How do you organize your workload? Can you describe what you do in this regard?"

"Why did you leave your last job?"

"Why do you want to make a change now?"

"What are you looking for in your next job that is missing from your current position?"

"What are your strongest assets that you bring to the job?"

(I don't recommend the often-asked, "What is your biggest weakness?" Most applicants will answer it with something similar to, "I work too hard" or "I expect too much from others because I expect so much from myself." You might want to try it just to see if you get a different response, though.)

"Do you prefer to work alone or with others?" Explain why.

"What about your work do you find most challenging?"

"Tell me about an experience you've had when you had to deal with a crisis or a great deal of stress in the workplace."

"Tell me about how you deal with people conflicts in the workplace. Can you describe any incidents you've handled?"

"In which of your jobs did you learn the most? Why?"

"What are your working conditions like at present? Would you be happy working in [describe facility]?"

"What is your reporting relationship like with your manager? How closely are you supervised now?"

"What is your current salary? What are you hoping to get in your next position?"

"With what other departments in your current organization do you have the most interaction? What is involved here, and how well do you get along with the staff members?"

"What about your job do you find the most unpleasant or difficult to do?"

"Can you tell me about any experience you've had in working under tight time constraints?"

"What is the one thing you would change about your current job if you had the power to do so?"

Add questions about your specific situation here:

_____

_____

_____

_____

_____

_____

_____

There are very few answers to these questions that are absolutely right or absolutely wrong. You have to learn how to evaluate the answers to judge whether they fit the profile of the individual you want in this particular position.

Future Plans and Aspirations

"What are your long-term career plans?"

"How do you think this position will help you in your plans for advancement?"

"What would be your ideal position?"

"Are you interested in moving up to management in the future, or are you more technically oriented?"

"What new responsibilities would you most like to take on if you are hired for this position?"

"Are you primarily looking for a growth opportunity or a change in working conditions?"

Candidates may be honest and candid about career aspirations and plans for the future, but it is also common for them to try to tailor their answers to what they believe is most compatible with the position offered. Inquire about their plans for the future, but remember that plans and circumstances are bound to change over time.

Executive Recruiting

Interviews of top-level executives differ greatly from the two other types because these candidates have already proved their worth. Skills, education, and practical experience are usually not the primary considerations here, since these candidates are generally accomplished enough to be able to demonstrate these achievements. In executive recruitment, you are looking for abilities in management, leadership, and technical and industry knowledge that fit with the needs of your own executive-level staff.

Executive-level interviews are generally more conversation-like than interviews for middle- and lower-level jobs. Once background information has been satisfactorily covered, questions should be asked that will encourage the candidate to share her management style and attitudes. You will not only want to talk about accomplishments but specifically how they came about. Here are questions that can get the conversation started:

"Tell me about the greatest change you've effected in your company."

"In what direction would you take this division were you to take this position?"

"What are the qualities you feel are most important in an employee? in a manager?"

"Why are you seeking to make a career change now?"

"What is unique about your approach to management?"

"What do you consider the most critical areas of control for which you are now responsible?"

"What do you do to earn respect and loyalty from your employees?"

"What are some of the biggest challenges facing this industry? this company?"

"How do you organize your staff? What levels of supervision are followed?"

Add your own questions for an executive in your industry:

_____

_____

_____

_____

_____

_____

It can be difficult to uncover unique qualities of the individual, as the following anecdote shows:

A candidate for an executive position came to be interviewed. The candidate was extremely accomplished, and the interviewer knew that the financial division of which he was currently vice-president had flourished. An executive search firm had recommended this candidate and had provided references and background information that promised he was the very best. The interviewer fully expected to be satisfied with the candidate and looked forward to talking to him. The interview started easily enough, but shortly after it began, he started to have his doubts.

Interviewer: How did you decide to go on to graduate school?

Candidate: Well, I really didn't know what else to do, so I just decided to try it.

Interviewer: Well, you've certainly accomplished a great deal since then. What would you say you are most proud of?

Candidate: I never thought about it.

Interviewer: Hmm, I see. What do you find most challenging in your current position?

Candidate: Oh, you know, day-to-day things can be as challenging as long-range projects.

The interviewer was about to give up when he realized that every question he had asked had been about the candidate himself. He decided to try to phrase a question differently.

Interviewer: I was told that you had really effected a financial turnaround in your company. How did that happen?

And he was off. Once the interviewer asked the candidate about a specific achievement, the candidate was able to articulate exactly what he had done, in the process demonstrating just how brilliant he was in his field. He was, of course, offered the position.

DID YOU ASK IT?

It is easy to get sidetracked when talking to an interesting candidate and find out later that you failed to ask some very basic but critical questions during the interview. Following are some questions you must be sure not to overlook. Add your own at the end concerning your specific business:

☐ Does the applicant have the basic requirements of the job, including education, experience, and technical ability?

☐ Can the applicant start when he or she is
needed?

☐ Is the applicant able to work the time required
for the job?

☐ Is the applicant's work style or methodology
compatible with your own and that of your
staff's?

☐ Will the applicant be comfortable working in
the available space?

☐ _____

☐ _____

☐ _____

☐ _____

CHAPTER 6

GETTING ANSWERS TO TOUGH QUESTIONS

"What is your salary requirement?"
"What do you like least about your occupation?"
"Why did you leave your last place of employment?"
"What are your expectations for your next job?"
"What are the qualities you look for in an employer or
  a manager?"

These questions are all reasonable to ask in an interview, and if the applicant answered them honestly, you would have gotten some very useful information. Usually, however, the answers to each of the questions are likely to be evasive or incomplete. Or you might not even get an answer.

It's not unusual for job applicants to be hesitant to commit to anything definite, such as salary requirement or job expectations. In fact, the word *requirement* when asked in a question such as, "Is working independently a requirement of a job for you?" can cause an applicant to retract statements already made in order to appear to be well-suited for the position. Similarly, questions that seem to push an applicant to speak negatively about a former employer or work experience can put the applicant on the defensive and cause her to respond evasively.

THE THREE R's

There are ways to obtain information that the applicant appears reluctant to divulge. They can be called the three R's

The three R's of interviewing: *repeat, rephrase, require.*

of interviewing: repeat, rephrase, require. Some circumstances call for using just one or two steps, and others may need all three:

1. *Repeat the question.* When an applicant tries to avoid answering your question, try repeating it. Sometimes she is so intent on imparting a specific item of information that she doesn't stop to listen to exactly what you are asking.
2. *Rephrase.* If repeating doesn't get a response, rephrase the question so that it is not as threatening to the applicant. Adding some qualifers such as, "I know it's a difficult question," or "I can appreciate why you might hesitate to answer, but . . ." can soften the impact of your question.
3. *Require.* Finally, you may need to require the applicant to answer the question.

Suppose you need to know the applicant's salary requirement. The following exchange covers the three R's:

Interviewer: What salary do you require in order to accept this position?

Applicant: That's hard to say. Of course, there are so many things to consider, and not the least important is the job itself. I'm really looking for a position that gives me an opportunity to increase my skills and that has room for me to grow as I improve.

Interviewer [*repeating*]: I appreciate that, but I imagine you do have an amount in mind that you would need in order to accept the job. What would that figure be?

Applicant: Well, as I said before, it really depends on the whole compensation package.

Interviewer [*rephrasing*]: And what would you think is a fair compensation package for you, for this particular position?

Applicant: I'm really not sure at this point. I think I need to know more about the position before I can make that determination.

Interviewer [*requiring*]: I understand your reluctance to commit yourself to a figure, but I do need to know if we are in the same ballpark in order to continue with this interview. I don't want to waste your time if there is no chance of a match. Take a few moments to think about it now, please.

At that point, the applicant has little choice, but to name the salary requirement that he probably has in mind from the start of the interview. Assuming that it is in the range you are offering, you can then continue the interview.

Some of the other questions that applicants stumble over are those that seem to ask them to speak to the negative. Most applicants like to keep interviews upbeat and positive. Rephrasing these questions and then encouraging the applicant to continue by practicing active listening can coax the information from even a closed-mouthed applicant. Here's an example of how it works:

Interviewer: What is it about your job now that makes you want to leave? Are you unhappy there?

Applicant: Oh no, it's not that. I just feel I'm ready to move on to more responsibility and a larger opportunity. This position seems to be just what I'm looking for. I really wanted a position in which I could use my technical skills and yet interact with people more.

Interviewer: Which of those opportunities does your present job fail to offer you

Applicant: Well, I do mostly technical work. I don't get a chance to work with users much.

Interviewer: And you find that frustrating?

Applicant: Well, it's just that I know I'm very good at explaining things. When I do get the chance to work directly with users, it always goes very well. That's why I was attracted to this position. You stated that you wanted someone with both types of skills.

Interviewer: Why do you think you wouldn't be able to increase your working with users in your present position, especially since you say it's been successful when it happens?

Applicant: That's just not the way it works there. Everything goes through the department manager. Staff members deal directly with the users only when he's away. I don't see that changing at all.

Interviewer: So, you're unhappy about that type of management structure then?

[*Finally, the applicant is ready to reveal why she wants to leave her present job.*]

Applicant: Well, to be honest, I find it stifling. I really need to be in an environment that allows me some more responsibility for what I do.

Interviewer: That's good to know. I believe we do share your philosophy on that.

In this example, it took a bit of digging to find out that the applicant was really looking for two changes: greater responsibility and a different type of manager. It is doubtful that the applicant would have revealed this information had it not been coaxed out of her. Note that each question the interviewer asked is based on information supplied by the applicant's answers. The interviewer is using active listening to its best advantage in this manner. (We will explore active listening in greater detail in the next chapter.) The interviewer rewarded the applicant by reacting positively to her "confession." This response is likely to encourage the applicant to continue being more open, thereby giving the interviewer more insight into what type of employee the applicant might be.

HOW TO USE SILENCE

If you are having a hard time getting an answer to a question from an applicant, you may choose to stonewall and see if your silence or curt responses can bring forth an answer. Most applicants find silence uncomfortable and seek to fill it to keep the interview going. Here's how it might work:

Interviewer: What do you think you can get from this position that will give you the satisfaction you are seeking?

Applicant: Oh, I think this job would be great for me. The description is exactly what I'd like to do.

Interviewer: Did you not feel that way about your present job when you decided to accept that position?

Applicant: No, not really.

Interviewer: Why was that different?

Applicant: Well, it was a different type of situation.

Interviewer: [*remains silent while looking up and making eye contact, seeking further explanation*]

Applicant: At that time I was mostly looking to get started. I really needed my first stepping-stone.

Interviewer: And now?

Applicant: Now I feel that I have the experience to offer you and that this is the type of job in which I could be happy. I'm looking for a place where I can stay and grow. I have a lot of different responsibilities in my present job, and I know that my interest—and I believe my talent—is in doing the work that this position calls for. I'm ready to specialize, so to speak, and my current company does not have that kind of opportunity.

DRAWING OUT QUIET TYPES

Sometimes an applicant is not evasive intentionally but just doesn't offer the information you need to make a fair judgment. Perhaps the applicant is afraid to reveal too much and feels that the less said, the better. You can draw this person out by paraphrasing what has been said and also by acting attentive and interested and requesting further details. Here's an example of how to interview a candidate for a secretarial position who is reticent to offer much information about herself:

A quieter candidate is not necessarily someone with less to brag about.

Interviewer: Tell me about your present position. What are your responsibilities?

Applicant: Oh, it's pretty much your basic secretarial duties. There are three managers who share my services.

Interviewer: That must keep you busy.

Applicant: Yes, I suppose you could say that.

Interviewer: [*realizing that the information will have to be pulled from this candidate*] Can you tell me how you manage to keep up with the needs of three managers? Do they all have similar workloads for you to contend with?

Applicant: Well, actually, one of the managers gives me more work than the other two.

Interviewer: Do you have any trouble keeping it all straight? It sounds like a big job.

Applicant: Actually, I've devised a system of my own to keep things organized. If I stick to that, I don't have much trouble.

Interviewer: Really, that sounds great. Tell me about it.

Applicant: Well, I just keep a log of everything.

Interviewer: And?

Applicant: I organize the work according to type and priority.

Interviewer: And how does that help you?

Applicant: Well, I find that by doing similar types of work together, I save time and energy. Not only do I do work by priority, but the managers and I have come to an understanding about this as well. They accept that I understand what is important and also that I will do my best to complete my assignments. They also accept that since I am one person working for three, there will be times when they will have to wait for something to be done.

Interviewer: You seem to have a strong sense of responsibility and a good understanding of the business your managers carry out.

Applicant: Oh, I think most secretaries do.

Interviewer: Only the good ones.

If the interviewer had not chosen to delve into this applicant's experience, it is doubtful that she would have made such a good impression.

Some candidates boldly boast about their accomplishments, but quieter candidates do not necessarily have less to brag about. They may not be completely comfortable talking about themselves, and if that is not essential to performing the job, you should make the effort to bring out the information these candidates are not sharing with you.

EVALUATING YOUR QUESTIONS

Most employment interviews should be limited in time. Except for a high executive position, forty-five minutes should be sufficient for a first interview. Therefore, it is important not to waste time on questions that do not give the applicant an opportunity to reveal important, evaluative information. Once you have had a fair amount of experience in interviewing, you will probably come up with several favorite questions that you ask all candidates, regardless of the position they are seeking. For example, many interviewers like to present a hypothetical situation to their job applicants and ask how they would resolve it. If you can, write down your favorite "challenging" questions for job applicants below:

_____

_____

_____

_____

_____

_____

_____

Now evaluate each question using the following checklist. If you cannot answer yes to one or more of the questions on the checklist, reconsider whether that question is truly worthwhile.

☐ Does the question ask something about the candidate you cannot learn from the resumé or job application?

☐ Does the question ask for specific information you need to evaluate whether the candidate is suited for this job?

☐ Does the question require the candidate to share opinions and ideas with you?

☐ Does the question ask the candidate to demonstrate knowledge, skills, or practical experience?

☐ Does the question require the candidate to reveal information about his work style or how he functions in the workplace?

CHAPTER 7

HOW TO LISTEN

Deciding upon and then asking the right questions of job applicants is the first important part in the equation that adds up to conducting a successful job interview. Listening to what is said and learning how to interpret what you hear is the second part.

Do you ever find yourself engaging in any of the following practices in an interview:

- You ask a question and then go on to the next without waiting for a complete answer.
- You anticipate what the answer to your question will be and then fail to listen if and when a different answer is given.
- You persist in asking a list of questions in a set order, regardless of the fact that the applicant reveals information that should be examined further.
- You allow yourself to be distracted from listening to the job applicant.
- You plan what to say next while the applicant is speaking.

Any or all of these practices can interfere with your making a fair evaluation and thus serve to sabotage your interview. Unless you know how to give your full attention to applicants and actively listen to what they are saying, the entire selection process might just as easily be held as a raffle instead of candidate interviews.

CLEAR AWAY DISTRACTIONS

It is imperative that a job interview be conducted in a private area without interruptions. You also need to be vigilant about other types of distractions, both external and internal. For example, are there items on your desk that you tend to play with—paper clips, maybe, or rubber bands? Remember that fidgeting is a distraction, and clear your desk of objects that will tempt you.

Internal distractions are more difficult to deal with. Are you worried about anything? (Of course, who isn't?) Don't allow a seemingly dull interview to be used as time to let your mind wander or dwell on your problems or concerns. Make your mind up that you are going to focus on what is said during the interview, because your most important order of business is to hire the best person for the job opening in your workplace.

BE PREPARED TO LISTEN

Consider these two different interviewers. Which one is ready to listen attentively?

Shari greets the job applicant warmly and shows her to her seat. Then she leans back in her chair, pushes back from the desk, and begins to ask questions. The applicant's resumé is in her hand, and she folds it several different ways as the conversation goes on.

Irving greets the job applicant warmly and shows her to her seat. Then he sits up in his chair and leans toward the applicant. He has marked several items on the applicant's resumé and has a pad on which he takes notes as the applicant speaks.

Clearly, it is Irving who is ready to listen to and learn about the job applicant he is interviewing. But Irving's exemplary interviewing behavior does not always come automatically.

You must be conscious of how you are presenting yourself and how you are preparing yourself to listen attentively. A good listener:

- Appears alert, yet with a relaxed posture
- Keeps comfortable eye contact with applicant
- Nods, smiles, and uses verbal cues to show interest and understanding
- Presents an open body posture: arms uncrossed, facing forward, head up
- Leans toward the applicant in a friendly manner
- Stays involved in the conversation by responding to what is said

WHAT ARE YOU LISTENING FOR?

The key to remember is the job itself.

Some interviewers may pride themselves in listening closely to all job applicants but may still err in what they are really listening for. The key to remember is the job itself. It is easy to get swayed by an interesting speaker who may be very pleasant and likable, but likable is not necessarily qualified. Successful interviewers must train themselves to listen for whether the applicant is suited for the available position.

One way to avoid getting off track by something the applicant says is to recognize what types of traps you are likely to fall into. For example, do you have a special interest or hobby that you also see evidenced in the applicant's resumé? Did the applicant come from the same town as you? Did you go to the same or neighboring schools? While a mention might serve as a simple icebreaker, you should leave it at that. Don't allow yourself to get involved in a nonwork-related discussion based on a mutual interest.

Before the interview begins, identify two categories of information you want to learn from the candidate:

1. Specific job skills, practical experience, and education essential to the job

2. How close this applicant is to the type of employee you feel is best for this particular job (that is, how the employee approaches the work process, how likely the candidate would be to work well with your current staff, and so forth)

As you ask questions designed to provide you with this information, listen carefully to the applicant. Then guide the applicant back to telling you essential information whenever you find the conversation straying to irrelevant material.

ACTIVE LISTENING TECHNIQUES

Active listening is actually a practice of paraphrasing and repeating.

Active listening is actually a practice of paraphrasing and repeating what a speaker is saying in order to keep the conversation on track, keep it going, and ensure that there are no misunderstandings. It is your way of helping both you and the applicant to stay focused on the subject. It can also be used to clarify some expressions that may be ambiguous. For example:

Applicant: Currently, I head a group of four people who respond to all customer inquiries that come into our business. We either give them help in solving the problem or direct them to someone else who can do so.

Interviewer: By "head" the group, do you mean that you supervise the work of the other three employees?

Applicant: Well, not officially. But I'm the most senior employee, and the others are always coming to me for help.

This applicant would have liked the interviewer to believe that he did supervise the others, but when he was asked directly, he had no choice but to explain the true situation. Although supervisory experience might not be a critical issue, the interviewer knows that she has to be alert if she is to get the true picture of this applicant's qualifications.

Active listening requires that you consider more than just the previous sentence by the applicant when phrasing your next question. Taking notes and remembering what has been said throughout the interview will allow you to ask questions that may give you very useful information.

CHECK IT OFF

One method that can be helpful in keeping on track is to check off the subjects that you want to cover as they are discussed, perhaps in conjunction with taking notes. Before the interview, prepare a short list of topics you want to cover. As they are discussed, check them off, jotting down the major points that were made. This list will prevent you from asking redundant questions, therefore helping you to make the best use of your time.

LISTEN FOR RED FLAGS

Many times, interviewees give you certain types of information without realizing it. Careful listeners can pick up red flag words or phrases that may tell a great deal about an applicant. This is particularly true in revealing prejudices or social attitudes that may be incompatible with your business, especially if the job involves dealing with the public or interacting with a culturally diverse work force. Use of any derogatory words about an ethnic or other group of people should send an immediate signal of alarm to your brain.

Other red flag words that may slip into conversations can reveal the applicant's attitudes about working, about management, and about how important certain aspects of a job may be to the applicant. The way an applicant describes current working conditions and refers to current coworkers and supervisors can offer you insights you perhaps were not intended to receive. You may choose to question the applicant when you hear a red flag phrase, or the use of the word may tell you so much that to ask a question would serve no additional purpose.

There are so many red flag phrases that it would be impossible to list them all. Here are a few examples. Write in the space provided what you think the use of the phrase tells you about the speaker and what, if anything, you would say to respond to the word or phrase.

Those types of people . . . _____

_____

_____

_____

It was very low-class . . . _____

_____

_____

_____

My last boss was very demanding . . . _____

_____

_____

_____

I was the only one who knew anything . . . _____

_____

_____

_____

I hate to say this about another person but . . . _____

_____

_____

_____

They were so difficult to get along with . . . _____

_____

_____

_____

We had a basic difference of opinion . . . _____

_____

_____

_____

I don't mean to generalize about a group of people, but . . .

_____

_____

_____

It was hard to concentrate while working under those conditions . . . _____

_____

_____

_____

CHAPTER 8

AVOIDING DISCRIMINATION DURING THE HIRING INTERVIEW

Which of the following questions may you legally ask a job applicant?

> "Do you have any children?"
> "Where are you from?"
> "What year did you graduate from college?"
> "What does your spouse do?"
> "Do you speak any foreign languages?"
> "Have you ever been arrested?"

If you answered "none," you have a good idea of what are legally defined to be discriminatory hiring questions in the United States. Asking discriminatory questions is an area in which it is very easy to get into trouble. Before asking any question of an applicant, mentally apply the following checklist in order to test its acceptability:

☐ It is directly related to the job.
☐ It does not request information regarding national origin.
☐ It does not request information regarding religion.
☐ It does not request information regarding marital status.
☐ It does not request information regarding parental status.

☐ It does not request information about personal activities.

☐ It does not request the applicant's age or information that would reveal the applicant's age.

☐ It does not request information regarding financial status.

Although it may not be apparent, the first question in the checklist, "It is directly related to the job," actually covers all of the other questions and any other restrictions there may be. However, even if you believe that you need certain information to make a decision on whether the applicant is well-suited for the position, you may not ask the applicant the question directly because it may violate equal employment opportunity laws or laws that protect the right to privacy. Applicants with physical and mental disabilities have specific rights during the hiring interview, which are defined in the Americans with Disabilities Act. We will discuss this in detail in Chapter 9.

WHAT'S AN INTERVIEWER TO DO?

Besides being aware of questions that are forbidden to ask during a hiring interview, the best way to defend yourself against having any problems in this area is to define the job and draw up a profile of the person you need. Then you can develop job-related questions that will give you the necessary information. This is not as easy as it may sound. Your profile of the best person for the job may inherently contain discriminatory preferences. Let's see how one interviewer, Dottie, learned how to translate her "needs" into a nondiscriminating applicant profile.

Dottie needs to employ a new public relations associate and has compiled the following profile of the perfect candidate.

- Between 25 and 35 years old
- Male or single woman without children

- College graduate
- Outgoing, assertive personality
- A minimum of four years' related experience
- Physically attractive
- No personal obligations that would interfere with business

Dottie then shows the profile to Stan, the human resources manager.

Dottie: How can I attract this type of candidate? I hate to waste my time interviewing people whom I know would not be right for this job.

Stan: Well, you've got some things on this wish list of yours that are clearly discriminatory. But before we get into those details, let me try to see how you came up with this profile. It may help us to rewrite it so that you can interview fairly and legally.

Tell me, what are the responsibilities of this employee that demand the restrictions you have set here? To begin with, why have you ruled out hiring a woman with children, which is, of course, illegal?

Dottie: First of all, the position requires a significant amount of travel.

Stan: Be more specific.

Dottie: The employee takes about three business trips a year. Each trip is three or four days long.

Stan: So wouldn't it be fair to say that travel is really not a big part of the job?

Dottie: Yes, but I think a woman with small children would have a problem with it.

Stan: I'm going to answer you by saying something you will have to repeat to yourself. It is actually the basis for practicing nondiscriminatory hiring—particularly involving women. This is it: The applicant's ability to deal with the requirements of the job regarding how they affect the applicant's home or personal life is essentially up to that individual to determine. You cannot know or inquire about the applicant's personal situation and how the individual would meet the requirements. You can only state the requirements and ask if the applicant will be able to meet them.

Dottie: So, you're saying that all I can do is inform the applicant about the travel requirements of the job?

Stan: Yes. It is up to the applicant to decide if that would be an acceptable part of the job. Now, what about this age range you've set? What are your reasons for wanting a person between ages 25 and 35?

Dottie: It's just that someone that age would be at just about the right stage of their career for this position. It's not so much a requirement as a guess at what age the ideal candidate would actually be.

Stan: I see. I understand your reasoning, and I agree that most applicants are likely to fall into that age range. Requirements for a certain amount of work-related experience would rule out very recent college graduates. Available salary might discourage an older professional, but the fact is that such a candidate is unlikely to apply for this job at all. However, by setting an arbitrary age as a requirement of the job, you are automatically discriminating against older employees who may have been away from the job market for some time or older applicants who are interested in changing fields. Age discrimination is illegal. The only legal question regarding age is to ask if the applicant is above the minimum working age for the position. In fact, you are not even permitted to ask what year the applicant graduated from school or college, because that would be construed as a way of determining the applicant's age.

Dottie: Just between you and me, I find that unfair. Why should I have to consider an older worker who's going to be looking toward retirement?

Stan: That's a very common sentiment, and certainly a major reason the law against age discrimination was enacted. But if you think about it, younger employees are just as likely to move on—if not for retirement, then for other opportunities. It is the rare employee who stays at one job for a lifetime, don't you agree?

Dottie: I suppose so. Well, what about my other requirements? Are there any laws against preferring to hire attractive, personable applicants?

Stan: Actually, no, although there have been lawsuits against employers who have fired employees who have perhaps gained a lot of weight and are no longer considered suitable to deal with the public. But there is no protection in the law for such employees, and no law against so-called discrimination in favor of more attractive candidates. However . . .

Dottie: I knew there would be a "however."

Stan: I must ask you again to define the requirement of the job rather than to suppose that only a certain physical type of person need apply. Although you may be legally able to choose the more attractive of two applicants, you may run the risk of discriminating against the physically handicapped when you set up these kinds of parameters, as perhaps you would consider a disability to be unattractive. You are also doing yourself a disservice by possibly disqualifying out of hand the best person for the position.

Dottie: So what do I do?

Stan: Reconsider your needs here. What you want is a public relations associate who can deal comfortably with the public. The employee must be able to interact well with strangers and present a positive image of the organization. Is that correct?

Dottie: Yes.

Stan: Then can you see that physical appearance is not necessarily a valid judge of ability to carry out these responsibilities?

Dottie: Yes. I do see what you mean. I've got to define the requirements for an employee as they directly relate to ability to perform the job.

Stan: Now you've got it!

Dottie is beginning to see what is required in order to hire without discrimination. She now has a better understanding of what she wants in a new employee and can identify the job–related requirements she may legally stipulate. Try writing a new employee profile for Dottie in the space provided:

_____

_____

_____

_____

_____

_____

_____

RACIAL, ETHNIC, AND RELIGIOUS DISCRIMINATION

Applicants are protected by law against discrimination based on race, national origin, and religion.

Job applicants are protected by law against discrimination or hiring preferences based on race, national origin, and religion. To this end, you may not ask an applicant about any of the following:

- Maiden name
- Country of origin
- Religion
- Religious organization memberships
- Religious customs or holidays observed
- References from a particular type of person, particularly a religious leader
- Citizenship

It is quite common for these items of information to come out during an employment interview, however, but if you handle the situation correctly you need not worry about being accused of discriminatory practices. For example, jobs that are scheduled for weekend hours may conflict with religious observations. Here is the correct way to cover this issue:

Interviewer: This position requires that you work every other Sunday. Are you able to meet that job requirement?

Applicant: No. I observe my religion on Sundays.

Interviewer: So you are saying that you cannot meet the job requirement of working on Sundays?

Applicant: I'm afraid so.

You should then write down, as documentation, "Applicant unable to work on Sundays." *Do not include that the reason is because of religious observance.*

Even if working on Sundays is a valid requirement of the job, if that is the only reason you choose not to hire an applicant, you may be guilty of religious discrimination. Depending on the size of your business (the larger the business, the greater your obligation), you could be required to make a reasonable effort to accommodate this candidate's religious observances. Therefore, even if you do not ask an applicant's religion, it could become an issue to contend with.

Laws against asking an applicant her maiden name are meant to protect against discrimination over national origin and also marital status. One legitimate reason to know an applicant's maiden name is to check references. However, you may not ask for the name directly. You can, after checking references unsuccessfully, say to the applicant, "The reference you gave did not know you. Is there an explanation for this?" At that point, the applicant will probably realize she needs to offer her maiden name. In terms of checking educational background, you can make inquiries of schools based on an applicant's social security number, which you can request on an employment application.

National origin privacy and citizenship status are protected by law. However, you must ask each applicant if he or she is legally permitted to work in the United States and if the applicant is prepared to show proof thereof within three days of employment, in accordance with the Immigration Reform and Control Act of 1986.

The right to privacy prevents you from asking many questions that you might consider innocent.

The right to privacy prevents you from asking many questions that you might otherwise consider innocent. In order to be legitimate, the question must relate to the candidate's ability to perform the job. Any questions asked "in order to get to know the candidate better" run the risk of being discriminatory. There are several cases in which you can ask about a subject, but only in a specific way—for example:

You may not ask: "What is your native language? How did you learn a foreign language?"
You may ask: "As required for the position, do you speak French? With what degree of fluency do you speak it?"

You may not ask: "Have you ever served in the military of any country? What kind of discharge did you receive?"
You may ask: "Have you ever served in the U.S. military? What duties did you perform while in service?"

You may not ask: "Who is your closest relative? How many dependents do you have?"
You may ask: "Do you have any relatives already employed by this company?"

Take the following test to see how well you understand discrimination laws.

DO YOU KNOW THE LAW?

Mark each question **L** for "legal" or **I** for "illegal."

_____ 1. Are you married?
_____ 2. Do you need time to make child care arrangements?
_____ 3. Have you ever been convicted of a felony?
_____ 4. Do you have any disabilities?
_____ 5. Where were you born?

_____ 6. What does your spouse do for a living?

_____ 7. Do you own your own home?

_____ 8. Do you anticipate the commute to be difficult?

_____ 9. What professional or business organization do you belong to that might enhance your ability to perform this job?

_____ 10. Do you belong to the country club in your town?

Answers: (1) **I**; (2) **I**; (3) **L**; (4) **I**; (5) **I**; (6) **I**; (7) **I**; (8) **L**; (9) **L**; (10) **I**.

CHAPTER 9

INTERVIEWING THE DISABLED

The Americans with Disabilities Act (ADA), enacted in July, 1992, has made a big difference in how physically and mentally disabled job applicants may be interviewed. In addition to limiting questions an interviewer may ask, it also requires that the potential employer actively seek to accommodate an applicant whose only disqualification is a physical inability to perform a given task or, perhaps more significant, perform a task in the same manner as it has traditionally been done. The phrase used in the legislation is "reasonable accommodation"; we look at what this means later in this chapter.

It is not unusual for interviewers facing a session with a disabled candidate to worry that they will make a mistake that could result in a lawsuit.

WHAT DO I DO?

The first impact of the ADA that managers and interviewers may feel is an increase in disabled people applying for job openings. The ADA was written to encourage this segment of the population to assert itself and pursue the right to be self-supporting and integrated into the workplace alongside more able-bodied coworkers. It is not unusual for interviewers facing a session with a disabled candidate to worry that they will make an incriminating mistake that could result in lawsuits or fines against the company. It may allay your concern to realize that the spirit of the ADA is essentially the same as the other laws in place against discrimination in hiring: All questions asked of a disabled applicant must directly address the individual's competence to perform the job. In addition, just as in the case of the applicant whose religious observance might obligate the company to adjust the position or work hours so as not to interfere with the applicant's religion, the company may be obligated to make specific accommodations to allow the applicant to perform the job responsibilities.

Similarly, just as it is not up to the interviewer to determine that an applicant with young children would not be able to perform the job, the interviewer cannot assume, by either advance knowledge of a disability or by observation, that a disability will prevent an applicant's being able to do the job. Your role is to describe the duties of the job and ask the applicant only, "Do you foresee any problems in performing any of the responsibilities I have detailed?"

To back up a little, it is understandable that you may be so nervous about violating the ADA that you begin by questioning the applicant about her ability to perform specific job functions, but this in itself can be said to be discriminatory. Begin an interview with a disabled candidate in the same manner as you would any other job applicant. Explore the applicant's qualifications, educational background, and related work experience. Learn all you can first about what qualifies the individual to apply for the job. Try to ignore what you perceive as a problem that limits the applicant and concentrate on the positive qualities he or she has. A common complaint voiced by persons with disabilities is that other people tend to define them by their disabilities. Try to look at the applicant not as "a paraplegic computer programmer" but as "John, a computer programmer with three years' related experience."

Learn all you can first about what qualifies the individual to apply for the job.

ELIMINATING OBSTACLES

Compliance with the ADA requires more than following a set of guidelines about legal and illegal questions and parameters on what is considered to be reasonable accommodation for an employer to make for a disabled employee. True compliance means eliminating physical and mental barriers that prevent disabled employees from entering the workplace. Therefore, as an interviewer, you can begin the process at the very start: with the writing of the job description for a vacant position.

Most often, job decriptions for open positions are heavily based on what was done by the previous employee holding that position. Since it is highly unlikely that person had a physical disability, the job description may be inherently discriminatory. You can change it by:

- Writing job descriptions that focus on the tasks required, not on the method by which they have always been done
- Requiring specific results, not skills
- Eliminating terminology that mentions specific physical capabilities, unless it can be said to be a bona-fide occupational qualification, which is a requirement that may appear discriminatory but can be justified as a business necessity
- Determining if a physically demanding task currently carried out by the individual in that position may be taken over by another coworker without creating any problems within the department, thus clearing the way in advance for a disabled applicant

Searching for a new employee requires that you prepare a profile of your ideal candidate. The ADA requires that you broaden that profile to include the possibility that the ideal candidate may have a disability.

CONDUCTING THE INTERVIEW

The sequence of the questions you ask can determine whether you have acted in compliance with the ADA. An appropriate sequence would be:

1. Discuss the applicant's qualifications, work experience, and job aspirations and interests.

2. Review the essential functions of the position and the basic requirements (which are the same for all applicants).
3. Ask if the applicant anticipates any difficulties doing the job. If the answer is yes, ask the applicant to be more specific. Wait for him to volunteer information about a disability; then assure him that the company has a policy of nondiscrimination.
4. Go through the reasonable accommodation process with the applicant.
5. Conclude the interview by assuring the applicant that the hiring decision will not be affected by the need for a reasonable accommodation.

WHAT IS A REASONABLE ACCOMMODATION?

A reasonable accommodation may be defined as an adjustment the company is required to make in order for a qualified applicant to perform a job function—for example:

- Structural changes to make the facility wheelchair accessible.
- An allowance of flexible hours so that the employee might avoid rush-hour travel.
- Job restructuring to reassign nonessential tasks that an applicant's disability might preclude.
- Providing special equipment or devices.
- Providing support staff. Larger firms, for example, may be obligated to provide readers or interpreters for blind or deaf employees.

Every interviewer must be prepared to go through the reasonable accommodation process with a job applicant. My advice is to proceed cautiously and allow the applicant to take the lead in explaining her disability. Never assume the applicant cannot perform a given task. Instead, ask, "How would you do . . . ?"

There are four steps to the reasonable accommodation process:

1. Analyze the position to determine its purpose and its essential functions. Decide what results you expect the employee to accomplish.
2. Discuss with the applicant how she feels the disability will limit her ability to perform these essential functions.
3. Consider together what possible accommodations could be made to eliminate these barriers.
4. In consultation with the applicant, select the accommodation that best serves both parties.

Let's look at an example of how Richard went through the reasonable accommodation process with Mario, a computer programmer who uses a wheelchair. After they have discussed Mario's job qualifications and Richard has delineated the responsibilities of the job, Mario expresses concern about the physical layout of the department:

Mario: I noticed coming through here that some of the hallways are rather narrow. I had some trouble getting my chair around packages and equipment that were left in the hallways. Is the office always kept like that?

Richard: No, but that does happen on occasion. But I think we can come up with a solution to that problem. Do you have any ideas?

Mario: Well, one way I know to keep halls free of clutter that would present a barrier is to designate an area for packages and spare equipment. You would have to make it a rule, I'm afraid.

Richard: I don't think that would be a problem. That's an accommodation we could make quite easily.

Mario: That would be great. The only other request I would make regarding my use of a wheelchair is that I would greatly appreciate being located near the fire exit and the rest room, which I see are on the south end of the floor.

Richard: I believe that could be arranged. Thank you for being open with me about your concerns, Mario. We can work these details out together.

Although you may say that Mario needed only minor adjustments, this example points out that with the passage of the ADA, the fact that hallways are too cluttered for wheelchair use is no longer an excuse. Instead, it has become the responsibility of the employer to see that the hallways are kept clear of obstacles. The obligation to accommodate has shifted from the disabled individual to company management.

The question of office location may seem simple but could be problematic to a manager who is not willing to be accommodating to a disabled employee. Although location and size of workplaces and offices may have status and political implications, it is certainly a reasonable accommodation to situate a wheelchair user nearby a fire exit. In such cases, it may take a little flexibility for others to adjust to the circumstances.

THINK BEFORE YOU SPEAK

If you are not acquainted with people with physical disabilities, it is not uncommon to speak in ways that could be offensive. The following do's and don't's offer some sensitivity guidelines:

- **Don't** express surprise at how well or how "normal" the applicant functions.
- **Don't** make generalizations about the disabled.
- **Don't** speak louder to a deaf person.
- **Don't** tell jokes about the disabled.
- **Don't** share stories about relatives or friends who are disabled.
- **Do** offer assistance if it seems appropriate, but wait until your offer is accepted before acting.
- **Do** allow for the extra time it may need a disabled

candidate to travel or to fill in forms or answer questions.

- **Do** use a normal speech and language. For example, don't be self-conscious to tell a blind person that it was "nice to see you."
- **Do** try to seat yourself at eye level with someone in a wheelchair.
- **Do** realize that the applicant is also an adult and capable of having both good and bad work experiences, just as any other applicant would be.

Finally, stop before you:

- Ask an applicant how she acquired the disability.
- Ask a disabled applicant personal questions.
- Ask a disabled applicant to reveal the full extent of his limitations. You may ask only about ability to perform essential job functions.
- Assume a disabled applicant will not be able to handle a specific task.
- Assume your employees will have trouble adjusting to working with a disabled applicant.
- Assume hiring a disabled applicant will be an undue burden on yourself and your staff.

CHAPTER 10

IT'S YOUR
TURN TO TALK

Up until now, we've concentrated on how to ask questions and listen to answers so that you can get all the information you need to make the best hiring decision. However, as an interviewer you are also responsible for providing information to each job applicant, for any applicant you select will also have to make a decision on whether to accept the job you offer.

With the exception, perhaps, of those interviews in which you immediately ascertain that the applicant is unsuitable, during every job interview with a potential employee you must share the following information:

- Job title and rank within department
- Job responsibilities
- Work hours
- Expected travel and overtime
- Potential for advancement and what is required for promotion consideration
- Salary range for position
- Physical working conditions available (don't surprise new employees with tiny or shared working quarters)
- Starting date required (if not negotiable)
- Company policy of nondiscrimination

In addition, there are probably specific facts about your company or the job in question that would be important to share with a potential employee. Use the space below to add this to your list:

_____

_____

_____

_____

_____

_____

BE HONEST

Don't allow pride to result in false exaggeration.

We all want to put ourselves and our company in the best light possible when interviewing potential employees, but don't allow pride to result in false exaggeration. You have prepared for this interview by defining the job responsibilities. Even if you are convinced of an applicant's ability to perform all tasks, you must still describe precisely what the job entails on a day-to-day basis.

Every individual who begins a new job hopes to find the work and the people agreeable and opportunity for advancement to be present. If you raise an applicant's expectations to unrealistic proportions by promising responsibilities and opportunites that do not exist, you are setting the scene for having an unhappy, frustrated employee who will probably leave at the first chance.

Job titles can be especially deceiving, and some managers create them specifically for that purpose. Avoid the temptation to allow an applicant to assume that the job title indicates certain job functions and privileges.

We recommend that you describe the position in general terms at the beginning of the interview, but save the detailed information for later. In this way, the applicant will not be able to tailor his or her answers to meet your exact needs.

ENDING THE INTERVIEW

Give the candidate the chance to ask you additional questions.

Toward the end of the interview, give the candidate the chance to ask you questions. If you do not know the answer to something asked, say so, and make a note of it so that you will be better prepared the next time.

Don't look at this as a time to relax and rest your listening sensors. The questions an applicant asks can be just as interesting and informative as the answers given to your own questions. What did the applicant most want to find out about? Compensation? Potential for advancement? Vacation? Working overtime?

At this time, you should tell the applicant what the next step in the interview process will be. The following statements will all serve to bring an interview to an end gracefully. You may want to prepare several different types of exit lines in advance to guard against an awkward moment in which the applicant is not sure whether he is expected to stay or go. You may be noncommittal, promising, or painfully honest; the choice is yours. However, if you are absolutely certain that the applicant will not be considered any further, do him the courtesy of telling him at the conclusion of the interview. In fact, if it does take longer to eliminate a candidate from consideration, the best practice is to call or send a brief note stating that another candidate has been selected. As disappointing as it is to receive such a message, waiting and hoping for a call that never comes is far more painful to endure.

Example 1: Thank you for coming and talking to me. We are going to be interviewing some more candidates for the position and expect to request second interviews by the end of next week.

Example 2: It was very nice to meet you. We are going to try to make a hiring decision within the next two weeks.

Example 3: I enjoyed our meeting very much. I have some more interviews to conduct, but I suspect I will be calling you to make arrangements for further discussion. You can expect to hear from me next week.

Example 4: Thank you for coming. Your qualifications impressed me a great deal. You will definitely be considered as one of the leading candidates for this position. When we have finished these preliminary interviews, we will make arrangements for a second meeting if you are still interested.

Example 5: Thank you for coming. I'm afraid that you do not have the required qualifications for this position. We would like to keep your resumé on file, however, should a more suitable position become available.

CHAPTER 11

FOLLOW-UP AND FINAL SELECTION

Take advantage of the situation to reassess the candidate. It's your last chance to avoid making a costly mistake.

No matter how thorough an interview you manage to conduct, you will undoubtedly want to call one or two candidates back for a second meeting before making your final decision. It is natural for you to let your guard down at this point. After all, your mind is almost completely made up; you're now just asking the candidate to return for a second look to confirm that this is the right person for the job. Instead, take advantage of the situation to reassess the candidate. It's your last chance to avoid making a costly mistake.

Follow-up interviews have several advantages that can allow you better to evaluate an applicant's suitability for the job:

- You have already determined the candidate has the necessary education and related work experience.
- You have a positive feeling about the candidate's work attitude and style.
- The candidate knows more about your organization and is demonstrating genuine interest by returning for a second meeting.
- You have had time to think about the candidate's answers to some of your previous questions and can formulate follow-up questions.
- You may choose to ask one or more coworkers to join in the meeting, so that you can get additional opinions.

WHAT ELSE IS DIFFERENT?

The pressure is on the candidate to obtain that job offer now.

A follow-up interview is often more intense than a first interview, especially for the job applicant. She knows that she has made a good impression and has the basic qualifications. Now the pressure is on to obtain that job offer, and she may be very anxious and eager to please you. You have to be able to make the candidate relax so that you can have an open conversation that will help you decide if the candidate is the best choice. Here are some tips on how to keep the follow-up interview focused:

1. *Get into details.* Now is the time to share with the applicant some of the details that will become his or her reality if the job is accepted. The difference is that now both you and the applicant know that the applicant is seriously being considered for the position. Discuss frankly the hours that will be expected to be worked and also any required travel.

2. *Review career goals.* Now that the applicant has had a chance to think about the job, discuss again how this position would fit into the candidate's career plans. What has the candidate done up until this point in order to reach individual goals? Where do you see the candidate moving to in the future? Is there compatibility between you?

3. *Introduce coworkers.* It can be quite helpful to introduce candidates to potential coworkers. This is a casual opportunity to talk and get a sense of the total organization. Both the candidate and the staff member may derive some valuable insight from this experience. A tour of the workplace is strongly recommended. A new employee who has seen only the offices of upper managers or personnel may be sorely disappointed in his own workstation. It is best not to give such a surprise to someone after accepting the position.

4. *Get hypothetical.* A follow-up interview is the time to assuage any of your fears that the candidate may not be capable of doing the job. If you have doubts, try asking the applicant what he would do in a hypothetical situation.

Although this may have been done in a first interview, trying it again in a second interview allows you to evaluate the answer on a different basis—that of one of the finalists in your selection process.

5. *Tie up loose ends.* Prepare for the follow-up interview by reviewing the candidate's application, resumé, and the notes you took at the initial interview. Be ready to ask about anything that remains a question and is relevant to the job. Review also the job profile and employee profile, and compare the applicant's characteristics to these decisions.

6. *Answer questions.* The applicant has had time to think about the job and will probably have more questions. Give the applicant all the information about the job that you can. There is no point in trying to hide or disguise a situation that will be immediately apparent once the employee has taken the job. Your goal should be to find an employee who will be satisfied with the position—not to trick someone into an unsuitable situation.

Many years ago, a woman I know worked as a secretary for two advertising salesmen at a metropolitan newspaper. Her salary of $175 a week was a very fair one at that time. The two men were difficult to work for, and they tended to exaggerate the chances for advancement a secretary of theirs would have. After working for the men for about four months, the woman left for a better job. She was quite happy to leave—she was even taking a small pay cut to do it—but she couldn't help feeling sorry for the person who would replace her. As she was getting ready to leave, she heard one of the salesmen on the phone to personnel. "I want this one to get $200 a week," he said. "We can't keep going through secretaries every few months."

As strong a motivator as money can be, it cannot compensate for everything in a working situation. Our friend knew that the next secretary would not be happy there if she was told the same stories that she had been. The higher salary might make it harder for her to leave, but our friend knew that only a certain type of person would be able to be happy

in that job. It seemed clear that her former bosses were not
going to bother looking that hard in order to find such a
person.

INTERVIEWING IN A GROUP

You may choose to conduct a follow-up interview as a group
meeting. This group might consist of any combination of
different types of people, such as another manager, department members, a personnel representative, or a senior manager. Although the candidate might find this intimidating, it
can help you to conserve time and also to assess how the
applicant functions in a group setting. Here are some guidelines to help you avoid setting up a stress situation:

- Do advise the applicant in advance that he will be
  interviewed by more than one person.
- Do arrange seating in a round rather than angled
  configuration, so that candidate can make eye contact
  with all parties without turning his head quickly back
  and forth.
- Do decide in advance what role each participant in the
  group will play. Let one person ask technical questions, another broader-based questions, and so forth.
- Don't interrupt one another with questions, forcing
  the candidate to choose which person to answer.
- Don't argue or discuss among yourselves, leaving the
  applicant out of the conversation.
- Don't embarrass the applicant by pointing out an
  error in front of others.

MAKING YOUR CHOICE

Before making a hiring decision, make sure you have done
the following:

☐ Checked the applicant's references

☐ Explained the position honestly to the applicant

☐ Determined that the salary range is acceptable to the applicant

☐ Identified all requirements of education, experience, and technical ability

☐ Provided equal employment opportunity to minorities and disabled candidates

☐ Evaluated the applicant's ability to advance with the organization

In the end, your selection will be based on both objective and subjective factors. You can eliminate some candidates on the basis of experience, education, and the like without hesitation. But determining whether an employee has the personality or character that is right for the job and for the work group in question is more difficult. Using what you have learned in this book will make you a more skillful interviewer who understands what is involved in selecting an employee who will be an asset to the organization and, most important, right for the job.

LEAVE NO DOUBT

Don't suffer a breakdown in communications once you have decided to hire a job applicant. Follow a verbal job offer with a written letter setting out the job title, salary, and benefits you have agreed upon and the starting date you have set.

Finally, don't be afraid to show enthusiasm and warmth toward the new employee. Making a smart hiring decision is the first step you've taken in improving the quality of your department's work output. It is then up to you to foster a cooperative working relationship with the new employee that will serve you both well in the years to come.

NOTES

NOTES

NOTES

NOTES

NOTES